LANCASHIRE
COUNTRY RECIPES

COMPILED BY
ANN GOMAR

Published by Ravette Books Limited
3 Glenside Estate, Star Road
Partridge Green, Horsham,
Sussex RH13 8RA
(0403) 710392

Production: Oval Projects Ltd.
Cover design: Jim Wire
Typesetting: Repro-type
Printing & binding: Nørhaven A/S

All recipes are given in Imperial and Metric
weights and measures. Where measurements
are given in 'cups', these are American cups,
holding 8 fluid ounces.

The recipes contained in this book are traditional
and many have been compiled from archival sources.
Every effort has been made to ensure that the recipes
are correct.

Front cover: The Soup Pot & Lid with bronze
side handles is available from Coppershop of
Covent Garden, 48 Neal Street, London WC2.

RECIPES

MEAT, OFFAL and SAUSAGES

PASTIES

VEGETABLES

PUDDINGS

SWEETS

CAKES and BISCUITS

LANCASHIRE

Lancashire is a county of very differing regions — all of which have played a part in its traditional food.

The industrial history of Lancashire has been the biggest influence on the local cooking. Between about 1750 and 1850 Lancashire was one of the cradles of the industrial changes which were to transform life in England and indeed most of the rest of the world.

Textile manufacture started as early as the end of the 13th century. By the Middle Ages it was flourishing. Merchants bought raw wool to be spun and woven on hand spinning wheels and looms in the workers' cottages. The invention in the late 18th and early 19th century of the flying shuttle, the spinning jenny, the water frame, and the mule, revolutionised the cotton industry by taking it out of the home and into the mill. Many of the local dishes originated in farmhouses, but had to be adapted to city life when smallholders were forced to leave the country as they were no longer able to supplement their incomes by home spinning and weaving.

Hearty breakfasts were eaten by the industrial workers. Porridge, sometimes served with treacle, was popular, oatcakes, fried bread, and bacon and eggs with black pudding. Pies and pasties filled with cheese and onion, meat or fruit, or crusty local bread or rolls filled with homemade spreads, sausages or cooked ham, were taken to eat during a break in the long working day in the factory or down the mine. Today, a famous and favourite sandwich is the chip buttie — bread and butter filled with hot, fried potatoes.

Coal miners' wives made a special pasty, similar to the Cornish, but in a foot shape to fit into the tins in which the men carried their meal or 'snap'. These pasties, which could be filled with meat, fish, vegetables, egg, cheese, onions, or bacon sometimes moistened with a little beer, are called Lancashire Foot. A pair are known as foots, not feet.

Because many of the women worked in the mills and a good hot meal was needed quickly to feed the family on her return, stews like Black Dish or Lobscouse were left on the black coal range. A former mill worker says: "It was a simple matter to slip home and put on a large brown dish of hot pot in the oven by the fire, or a steamed pudding. These boil very slowly, but sometimes a neighbour would pop in to top up the water in the saucepan. The tradition was that the working men in the family were honoured with a steak and kidney pudding cooked in a dish. The children had to be content with one boiled in a 'rag'— a piece of linen kept for that purpose."

For economy all of an animal was used, providing local specialities like tripe and onions, black puddings and steak and cow-heel. Individual pig keeping was so popular that the story of the Pig o' t' wall is told about several Lancashire villages. Legend has it that owners put their pigs up on a wall to watch a band or procession going by!

Lancashire has its own cheese. It is crumbly and excellent for cooking, but also delicious with oatcakes. Sheep and cattle graze in the outstandingly beautiful Trough of Bowland, on the Lancashire Pennine hills, and Pendle in the Ribble Valley. Pendle Hill still retains an aura of mystery. It was from the villages and hamlets of this lovely region that the famous Lancashire witches were taken in 1612 to be tried and hung for sorcery at Lancaster Castle.

In Lancashire traditional food was especially prepared for festivals, such as Christmas, Easter and the Wakes. Hundreds of years ago a watch or wake was kept on the night before the anniversary of a local church's dedication to a saint. Gradually feasting was added to the celebrations, and eventually the word 'wake' was used to describe local fairs and the annual holiday Wakes Week when the mills and factories shut down. In medieval times the fair was a great occasion. People came from remote hamlets to join in the feasting, entertainment and fun of the fair, as well as to buy provisions, clothes and goods of all sorts from itinerant merchants. Some of the market days and fairs dating back to the 13th century were held in Liverpool, Preston, Lancaster, Clitheroe, Wigan, Newton, Manchester, Warrington, Farnworth, Rochdale, Bolton, Burnley, Ulverston and Dalton. Morris and clog dancing, brass bands and folk singing remain popular today.

In 1857 when Charles Dickins and Wilkie Collins toured the North of England visiting many inns and recording their adventures, they stayed at The Kings Arms in Market Street, Lancaster. The proprietor, Joseph Sly, a prominent Lancastrian businessman, served them with two little salmon trout, a brace of partridge, seven dishes of sweets, five dishes of dessert led off by a bowl of peaches, and in the centre an enormous bride cake. Bride cake is wedding cake, made from a rich fruit cake mixture such as that used in Simnel Cake. The custom of serving bride cake after dinner arose because of a ghost story associated with the inn. A young bride had been poisoned in the 'Bride's Chamber', and the murderer was hanged at Lancaster Gaol. It is recorded that Dickens stayed in the room, and slept well in the bed.

There is a proud heritage of home cooking in Lancashire, which has been handed down through the generations from grandmother, to mother and daughter. A love of High Tea and the importance of Sunday Tea probably account for the number of delicious cake recipes.

The spirit of friendliness and helpfulness is very much a part of Lancashire life, and visitors will be able to share in it as well as sample some of the delicious local fare.

'Let us go to the Mottram Wakes
Bonnie lassie, oh!
And I'll buy thee nuts and cake:
Bonnie lassie, oh!'

From the song *Mottram Wakes* by Samuel Cottrell
1799-1837, a spinner in a cotton mill at Stalybridge.

BARLEY SOUP

Serves 4

This hearty, cheap and nourishing soup originally comes from Ireland. Many Irish people have settled in Lancashire to live and work, so it is not surprising that some favourite recipes have crossed the Irish Sea.

8 lamb neck ends
1 cup of barley
4 carrots
1 onion
1 leek
2 pints (1.5 litres/ 4 cups) water

Put the barley in a basin and cover with cold water.

Leave to soak overnight. Drain.

Put the neck ends in a saucepan, and cover with cold water.

Bring to the boil and simmer for about 5 minutes.

Drain.

Peel and chop the vegetables.

Add them with the barley and 2 pints (1.15 litres/ 4 cups) fresh water to the neck ends in the saucepan.

Bring to the boil and simmer gently for about 4 hours.

If the soup becomes to thick add a little more water as required.

Eat the tender neck ends with the soup.

Serve with crusty bread.

PEA SOUP

Pea soup has been made since the Middle Ages, and was one of the most popular dishes to be sold from street barrows. Green or black peas could also be bought cooked by the cupful and were often eaten with vinegar. They were also sold at fairs or wakes.

Peas have been a favourite vegetable in Lancashire for many centuries. Boiled peas or peas fried in butter and seasoned with salt and pepper were always served on Care Sunday, the Sunday before Palm Sunday. The peas served on this day were known as Carlings.

8 oz (225 g) green split peas
2 pints (1.15 litres/ 4 cups) ham stock or water
1 onion
1 carrot
1 stick of celery
2 oz (50 g) bacon
1 oz (25 g) dripping
Salt and pepper
Bouquet garni
¼ pint (150 ml/ ⅔ cup) milk
2 fl oz (3 tablespoons/ ¼ cup) cream
Mint, chopped (optional)

Soak the peas in cold water for 12 hours.

Dice the onion, carrot, celery and bacon, and fry in the dripping for a few minutes.

Drain the peas and put in a large saucepan with the diced vegetables and bacon.

Pour on the stock and season to taste with salt and pepper.

Add the bouquet garni.

Bring to the boil, and simmer gently for about 2 hours or until the vegetables become a pulp.

Remove the bouquet garni.

Put the soup through a sieve or purée in an electric blender.

Before serving, re-heat the soup gently.

Add the milk.

Swirl in the cream just before serving the soup scattered with chopped mint.

PEA SOUP WITH LENTILS   Serves 4

The ribs in this soup make a tasty dish served separately with potatoes and green cabbage.

6 oz (175 g) dried peas
1 sheet of bacon ribs, chopped, or 1 ham shank
1 cup of lentils
4 carrots
1 onion
1 leek
4 potatoes (optional)

Soak the lentils and peas overnight, then drain.

Put the bacon ribs in a saucepan, and cover them with cold water.

Bring to the boil and simmer for about 5 minutes.

Drain.

Peel and chop the vegetables and add them with the lentils peas, and 2 pints (1.15 litres/ 4 cups) fresh water to the ribs in the saucepan.

Bring to the boil and simmer gently for about 4 hours.

Remove the ribs or ham shank before serving with crusty bread.

VEGETABLE BROTH WITH
SUET DUMPLINGS

For the broth:
8 oz (225 g) lentils
8 oz (225 g) dried spilt peas
1 leek
2 medium sized carrots
A few cabbage leaves
2½ pints (1.4 litres/ 5 cups) stock or water
Salt and pepper to taste

For the dumplings:
2 oz (50 g) shredded suet
4 oz (100 g) plain flour
Salt
Water or milk to mix
A little extra flour

To make the broth:

Soak the lentils and split peas in cold water overnight, then drain.

Peel and dice the carrots.

Wash and shred the cabbage leaves.

Wash the leek and chop into small pieces.

Put the lentils, peas and prepared vegetables into a large saucepan and cover 2½ pints (1.4 litres/ 5 cups) stock or cold water.

Season to taste with salt and pepper.

Bring to the boil, then simmer slowly for 2½-3 hours until all the ingredients are cooked and the soup is thick.

To make the dumplings:

Put the shredded suet, flour and salt into a bowl.

Mix with a little water or milk to a soft dough.

Form with the hands into small balls, rolling each one in flour.

Drop the dumplings into the simmering broth about 20 minutes before the end of cooking after which time they will be well risen and soft.

Serve the broth in bowls with the dumplings.

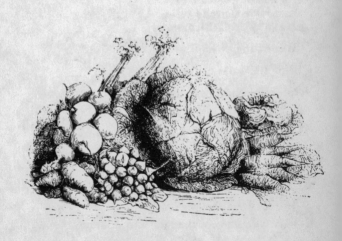

POTTED SHRIMPS FROM MORECOMBE BAY

Shrimps from Morecombe Bay are famous far beyond the county, and have been highly regarded for at least two centuries. Economical Lancashire housewives potted the surplus catch in clarified butter.

Potted shrimps are delicious served as a beginning to a meal, with brown bread and butter, on toast or plain biscuits as a cocktail savoury, or as a sandwich filling.

If you buy the shrimps from the fishmonger they will be already cooked, but if you catch them yourself, cooking them is quite easy.

For cooking the shrimps:
1 quart (1.15 litres/ 4 cups) of shrimps
Water to cover
Salt — allow ½ oz (15 g) to every pint (600ml/ 2½ cups) of water

For potting the shrimps:
1 quart (1.15 litres/ 4 cups) cooked and shelled shrimps
Salt and cayenne pepper
A pinch of ground cloves
Anchovy essence to taste
6 oz (175 g) clarified butter

To cook the shrimps:

Bring the water to the boil.

Put in the shrimps and boil for 5 minutes.

Drain and allow to cool.

Shell the shrimps.

To make clarified butter:

Heat slighly salted butter gently in a saucepan, stirring all the time until the liquid foams.

Cook without browning until the foaming stops.

Allow to stand for a few minutes, but not to solidify.

Strain, through muslin before using.

To pot the shrimps:

Melt 3 oz (75 g) of the clarified butter and stir in the salt, cayenne pepper, ground cloves and anchovy essence.

Put the shrimps in an ovenproof dish and add the seasoned melted butter.

Cook in a moderate oven for 20 minutes.

Remove the dish from the oven.

Strain the shrimps and reserve the butter.

When cool pack the shrimps tightly into small jars.

Pour the reserved melted butter over the shrimps.

Allow the butter to set.

Cover the shrimps with the remaining clarified butter, which should be about ¼ inch (5 mm) in thickness.

Potted shrimps must not be kept for more than a few days.

Oven: 350°F/180°C Gas Mark 4

KIPPER PATÉ

1 lb (450 g) kipper fillets
¼ pint (150 ml/ ⅔ cup) dry white wine
3 tablespoonsful of lemon juice
6 oz (175 g) unsalted butter
Salt and black pepper

Take the skin off the kipper fillets.

Put the fish in a shallow bowl.

Pour the wine over the fish, and leave to marinate for 3 to 4 hours.

Mash with a fork or blend in an electric mixer, the kipper fillets together with the wine and the lemon juice.

Season with salt and black pepper to taste.

Soften the butter and beat it into the mixture.

Pack the paté into a serving dish.

Serve with Melba toast.

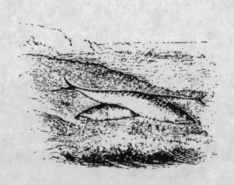

POACHED SALMON IN WHITE WINE WITH CUCUMBER GARNISH

Serves 4

4 salmon steaks
1 bay leaf
2 sprigs of mint
4 sprigs of parsley
Salt and cayenne pepper
A tumblerful of dry white wine
Juice of 1 lemon
1 cucumber

Put the salmon steaks into a large saucepan, so that they do not overlap.

Add the bay leaf, mint and parsley.

Sprinkle with salt and cayenne pepper to taste.

Peel and slice the cucumber.

Cover the fish with one or two layers of cucumber.

Add the white wine and lemon juice.

Simmer the fish very gently keeping the temperature below boiling point for about 25 minutes.

Remove the bay leaf, mint and parsley.

Reserve the fish liquor.

Arrange the salmon steaks on a serving dish, garnished with the cucumber.

Pour over the wine sauce and serve hot with green peas.

FISH AND CHIPS

Fish and Chip shops are very popular in the county. Here is a delicious recipe to try at home.

For the fish and chips:
1½ lbs (675 g) potatoes
1½ lbs (675 g) cod or haddock fillets
Salt and pepper
Batter
Lemon juice (optional)
Oil for deep frying

For the batter:
2 oz (50 g) plain flour
A pinch of salt
4 tablespoons (⅓ cup) water
2 teaspoons oil
1 egg

To make the batter:

Sieve the flour and salt into a bowl.

Make a well in the centre.

Gradually mix in the oil and water and beat until smooth.

Leave to rest while preparing the fish and chips.

Just before using the batter, separate the egg.

Whisk the white until dry and forming peaks.

Fold into the batter and use at once.

To make the fish and chips:

Peel and cut the potatoes into slices about ⅜ inch (1 cm) thick. Cut each slice into ⅜ inch (1 cm) sticks.

If not cooking the chips immediately, put them into a bowl and cover completely with cold water to prevent browning.

Cut the fish into four portions.

Wash and dry thoroughly on kitchen paper.

Season with salt, pepper and a little lemon juice.

Drain the chips and dry thoroughly on kitchen paper.

Put sufficient fat in a large frier (with a wire basket) to come three quarters of the way up the pan. Heat the oil to about 350°F/183°C.

If no thermometer is available, drop a 1 inch (2.5 cm) cube of bread into the fat. If it browns in 1 minute, the oil is ready.

Put about one third of the chips in the wire basket, and lower it carefully into the hot oil.

Cook until soft, but not brown.

Remove from pan, and drain on kitchen paper.

Repeat until all the chips are partially cooked.

Dip the fish into the batter to coat.

Put the fish into the wire basket and lower carefully into the reheated oil.

Fry for about 7 minutes until golden brown and cooked through.

Remove from the pan, drain on kitchen paper, and put the fish in a low oven to keep hot.

Put all the chips into the wire basket, lower carefully into the hot fat and fry until golden brown.

Drain on absorbent paper, and serve at once with the fish.

When cool, the oil can be strained and kept to use again.

BAKED TROUT WITH CREAM SAUCE

Serves 6

6 trout
2 lemons
7 fl oz (200 ml/ ¾ cup) single cream
3 oz (75 g) breadcrumbs
2 oz (50 g) butter
A little chopped parsley

Lay the cleaned and prepared trout in an ovenproof dish.

Squeeze the lemons and pour the juice over the fish.

Cover the dish with a foil lid and bake in a moderate oven for 15 minutes or until the fish are cooked.

Remove from the oven.

Gently heat the cream in a saucepan, and pour it over the fish.

Sprinkle on the breadcrumbs.

Melt the butter and pour this on the fish.

Put the dish under a hot grill to brown, and heat through.

Serve at once, garnished with chopped parsley.

Oven: 350°F/180°C Gas Mark 4

HONEYED ROAST TURKEY

Serves 8

Cooking a turkey in honey is popular in the north of England. The Romans are known to have roasted large birds, like swans, and herons, using this method.

The honey acts as a seal and prevents the turkey from drying during cooking, which it is inclined to do. When served the meat will be white and succulent, and the black skin crisp and tasty.

12 lb (5.5 kg) stuffed turkey
12 oz (350 g) thick honey
6 oz (175 g) butter

Put the stuffed turkey in a baking dish.

Melt the honey and butter in a saucepan, stirring occasionally to mix thoroughly.

Spoon the mixture over the bird.

Leave to stand for 30 minutes.

Spoon any honey mixture that has run into the dish over the bird.

Roast in a hot oven for 30 minutes.

Baste the turkey, which will have turned black, with any liquid honey mixture in the dish.

Reduce oven to moderate and cook for a further 30 minutes.

Baste again with any liquid in the dish.

Cover the bird with tin foil and cook for a further 2 hours.

About 20 minutes before the end of the cooking time, remove the foil to allow the skin to finish crisping.

Oven: 400°F/200°C Gas Mark 6
Reduce to: 350°F/180°C Gas Mark 4

HINDLE WAKES CHICKEN

Serves 6

It is said that this dish was first introduced to Lancashire by Flemish spinners who came to live and work in the Bolton region in the 12th century. In those days chickens were valued for egg-laying and only old and tough birds were cooked. So chickens were generally used in pies and puddings or boiled to make them tender.

This recipe for cold chicken stuffed with a prune mixture and served with lemon sauce became so popular that it was traditionally served during the annual Wakes Week — hence its name, which is thought to derive from 'Hen de la Wake' (Hen of the Wake) — hence Hindle Wakes.

A 4 lb (1.75 kg) boiling chicken

For the stuffing and garnish:
8 oz (225 g) prunes
6 prunes and parsley for decoration
1 onion
2 oz (50 g) fresh white breadcrumbs
1 oz (25 g) mixed dried herbs
1 oz (25 g) suet
A pinch of cinnamon
1 lemon
Salt and pepper
1 egg, beaten

For the chicken stock:
About 5 pints (3 litres/ 10 cups) chicken stock or water

For the lemon sauce:
1 oz (25 g) butter or margarine
1 oz (25 g) flour
½ pint (300 ml/1¼ cups) milk
7 fl oz (200 ml/ ¾ cup) chicken stock
¼ pint (150 ml/ ⅔ cups) double cream
1 lemon

To make the stuffing:

Soak all the prunes overnight.

Drain, and reserve 6 for decoration.

Chop the remainder.

14

Peel and chop the onion.

Put the breadcrumbs in a bowl. Stir in the chopped prunes, onion, suet, herbs, cinnamon and salt and pepper to taste.

Squeeze the lemon and blend the juice into the mixture.

Stir in the beaten egg to bind the stuffing.

To cook the chicken:

Put the stuffed and trussed chicken in a large saucepan and cover with the stock.

Bring slowly to the boil.

Put the lid on the saucepan, and simmer very gently for 2-3 hours or until tender.

When cool, take the chicken from the saucepan and remove the skin before putting it on a serving dish.

Reserve 7 fl oz (200 ml/ ¾ cup) of the stock for the sauce. (The remainder will make excellent chicken soup.)

To make the sauce:

Melt the butter or margarine in a saucepan.

Stir in the flour to make a roux and cook for a few minutes, stirring continuously.

Gradually stir in the milk and the chicken stock.

Cook until the sauce thickens. Season.

Grate the lemon rind finely and squeeze the juice.

Stir the rind and juice into the sauce and add the cream.

Allow the sauce to cool, then spoon it over the chicken to coat.

Decorate the chicken with halved prunes and chopped parsley before serving cold.

GOOSNARGH CHICKEN WITH WILD MUSHROOM SAUCE

Serves 4

FROM BROUGHTON PARK

Broughton Park, Preston, is a lovely old mansion set in its own woodland grounds and lawns. Built in 1891 it was originally an elegant home. In recent years it has become an hotel of character and atmosphere, with a reputation for excellence in food.

Paul Heathcote, Chef de Cuisine, uses corn fed chicken from Swainson House Farm, Goosnargh, for this recipe.

3.5 lb (1.5 kg) chicken
1 onion
Oil for frying
⅛ pint (4 tablespoons/ ⅓ cup) dry white wine
1 shallot (or 1 teaspoon chopped onion)
6 ozs (175 g) wild mushrooms — if not available, flat
**   and button mushrooms can be used, or if in summer**
**   try to obtain Scottish chanterelles**
½ pint (300 ml/ 1¼ cups) whipping cream
¼ pint (150 ml/ ⅔ cup) chicken stock
1 oz (25 g) butter

Take off the breasts and legs of the chicken.

Chop the carcass.

Put in a saucepan of cold water with half an onion.

Bring to the boil and simmer for 1 hour to make the stock.

Lightly pan fry the four pieces of chicken until golden brown on either side.

Put in a baking dish and cover with buttered paper.

Cook in a slow oven for 45 minutes or until cooked.

Put on a serving dish and keep warm.

Fry the chopped shallot (or onion) in the frying pan for about 1½ minutes until lightly cooked.

Add the white wine and boil to reduce by half.

Stir in the previously made chicken stock and reduce this by half.

Add the cream and mushrooms and reduce by half again.

When the sauce has thickened and is at the desired consistency, whisk in the butter.

Season with salt and pepper to taste.

Pour the sauce over the chicken and serve.

Oven: 325°F/160°C Gas Mark 3

PHEASANT IN PUFF PASTRY WITH WILD MUSHROOMS

FROM THE INN AT WHITEWELL   Serves 2

The Inn at Whitewell in the beautiful Hodder Valley of the Forest of Bowland is as renowned today for its good food and hospitality as its long and interesting history — dating back for at least 600 years. The house was formerly known as Whitewell Manor. For centuries a thriving market was held in the forecourt which attracted many people from the surrounding valleys and fells.

By 1612 Whitewell had become an inn where judges stopped overnight on their way to the famous trial of the Lancashire witches. The wretches accused of sorcery walked past it on their long journey to Lancaster Gaol, where they were found guilty and hanged. This is a favourite recipe from Head Chef, Geoffrey Beetlestone.

For the pheasant:
1 pheasant, filleted
1 oz (25 g) butter

For the wild mushroom duxelle:
5 oz (150 g) wild mushrooms — a mixture of trompets
   de mort, chanterelles and cepes, either fresh or dried.
   If the mushrooms are dried, soak in a little white
   wine or sherry before using.
1 medium onion
2 eggs
About 2 tablespoons of fresh breadcrumbs
1 oz (25 g) butter
Salt and pepper
A little tarragon
A little white wine or sherry, if required

For the pastry:
8 oz (225 g) puff pastry

To prepare the pheasant:

Draw either a hung or fresh pheasant.

Reserve the liver of the bird, after removing the bile sack.

Carefully take out the wish bone.

18

Cut off the wings at the joints.

Skin and remove the breast meat, one supreme at a time.

Melt 1 oz (25 g) butter in a pan, and season it with salt and pepper.

Fry the breasts to seal in the hot butter.

Remove from the pan and leave to cool.

To make the wild mushroom duxelle:

Chop the onion finely.

Cook in about ½-1 oz (15-25 g) butter in a saucepan with the lid on for about 2 minutes until soft.

Chop the mushrooms very finely, and add them to the onion.

Season with salt, pepper, and tarragon to taste.

Cook the mushroom and onion mixture for about 20 minutes on a low heat, stirring occasionally to prevent sticking.

When cooked, the mixture should be slightly moist.

Add 1 large tablespoonful of fresh breadcrumbs and cook for a further 2 minutes, stirring constantly.

Remove from the heat, and when half cool add one egg and mix together thoroughly to bind the mixture. If too wet, mix in a few more breadcrumbs taking care not to add too much. The mixture should taste of mushrooms not of bread. Allow to cool completely.

To make the pheasant in puff pastry:

Roll out on a floured board either homemade or bought puff pastry to an oblong about 10 inches x 5 inches (25 cm x 13 cm) and 3mm thick.

Cut the pastry in half to make two 5 inch x 5 inch (13 cm x 13 cm) squares.

Put a good amount of mushroom duxelle in the middle of each pastry square.

Cut the liver in half and put one piece each on top of the duxelle.

Put the pheasant breasts on top of the liver.

Beat the egg and use to dampen the edges of the pastry squares.

Take the opposite corners of one square and fold into the middle.

Seal together firmly.

Take the other pastry corners and fold likewise to make an envelope. Seal tighly. Repeat with the other pastry square.

Allow the pheasant in the pastry to cool in a refrigerator for about 30 minutes before cooking, if time permits.

Cook in a moderate oven for no more than 15 to 20 minutes.

Chicken liver may be used instead of game, and cultivated mushrooms instead of wild.

Serve with a rich game gravy made with the carcass and giblets.

Oven: 375°F/190°C Gas Mark 5

UNCLE FELIX'S WILD
BRAISED DUCK

Serves 2-3

1 prepared wild duck
Salt and black pepper
6 rashers streaky bacon
1 oz (25 g) butter
Bouquet garni
¾ pint (450 ml/ 2 cups) giblet stock
½ pint (300 ml/ 1¼ cups) thick brown stock
1 wineglassful of red wine

Season the prepared duck with the black pepper and salt.

Lay the rashers of bacon in the bottom of a saucepan and put the duck on top of them.

Add the butter.

Put the lid on the saucepan, and simmer the duck very gently for 15 minutes, turning it once half way through the cooking time.

Remove the duck and bacon but leave the fat in the saucepan.

Cut the duck up into joints, and the bacon in half.

Put the duck back into the saucepan, and fry it in the fat for a few minutes.

Stir in ¾ pint (450 ml/ 2 cups) of stock made with the giblets and ½ pint (300 ml/ 1¼ cups) of thick brown stock.

Add the bacon and the bouquet garni, and simmer for 45 minutes.

Add the wineglassful of red wine after 40 minutes of the cooking time.

Remove the bouquet garni before serving.

LANCASHIRE HOTPOT

This stew was traditionally cooked in a tall brown or white pot made of pottery, from which it was served. A real Lancashire Hotpot is not over-moist. Sometimes streaky bacon is laid on the top of the dish towards the end of the cooking time; another addition can be sliced black pudding. This was often added during the Second World War to eke out the meat. Oysters were used in the dish, but can be omitted if preferred. The traditional accompaniment to Lancashire Hotpot is pickled red cabbage.

6 middle neck lamb chops
6 oysters (optional)
3 lamb kidneys
8 oz (225 g) onions
1½ lbs (675 g) potatoes
Salt and pepper
½ pint (300 ml/ 1¼ cups) white stock (from a chicken stock cube if necessary) to give the traditional light colour
1 oz (25 g) dripping or lard

Trim any excess fat from the chops.

Skin and remove the core from the kidneys, and slice.

Peel and slice the potatoes and onions.

Fry the chops and kidneys on both sides in a frying pan in their own fat for a few minutes.

Put the chops in an ovenproof casserole.

Scrub the shells, open them and remove the oysters (or ask your fishmonger to open them).

Place an oyster on top of each chop.

Cover the chops with a layer of kidney, then the onions and potatoes, seasoning each layer with salt and pepper.

Continue with the layers, until all the ingredients are used, finishing with a layer of potatoes.

Pour on the stock.

Melt the dripping or lard in a saucepan.

Brush the potatoes over with the melted fat.

Cover the casserole with a lid or foil and bake in a moderate oven for 2 hours.

Remove the lid, and brown the potatoes for a further 20 minutes in a hot oven.

Oven: 325°F/160°C Gas Mark 3
Increase to: 425°F/220°C Gas Mark 7

STEWED STEAK AND COW-HEEL   Serves 6

12 oz (350 g) stewing steak
4 oz (100 g) lamb's kidney, skinned and cored
1 cow-heel, dressed and cooked by the butcher
1 onion
About 1 pint (600 ml/ 2½ cups) brown stock or water
Salt and pepper

Cut the meat and the cow-heel into small pieces.

Peel and chop the onion.

Put the steak, kidney, cow-heel and onion in a saucepan with sufficient stock or water to cover.

Season with salt and pepper.

Simmer gently for about 3 hours, or until tender.

Remove all meat from the heel and serve the stew hot with potatoes and vegetables.

If preferred the stewed meat and onion can be put into a pie dish and covered with a lid of pastry made from 8 oz (225 g) shortcrust pastry, brushed with beaten egg and baked for 1 hour in a moderate oven.

Pour any left-over stew into a mould or small basin and leave to set. The resulting brawn can be sliced and eaten in sandwiches, or with a salad.

Oven: 350°F/180°C Gas Mark 4

STEAK AND KIDNEY PIE

Serves 4

This pie is found, sometimes with regional differences, throughout the country. Oysters are a popular addition in the north. If liked, add about six chopped oysters to the meat before the pastry lid goes on.

12 oz (350 g) stewing steak
4 oz (100 g) lamb's or ox kidney
2 oz (50 g) seasoned flour
2 tablespoons vegetable oil
2 medium onions
About ½ pint (300 ml/ 1¼ cups) brown stock
Salt and pepper
8 oz (225 g) shortcrust or puff pastry
Beaten egg to glaze

Cut the stewing steak into small pieces.

Remove the skin and core, and cut up the kidney.

Roll the meat in the seasoned flour.

Heat the oil in a frying pan, and fry the meat and onions until brown.

Put the meat and onions into a saucepan and add sufficient stock to cover. Season with salt and pepper.

Bring to the boil, cover and simmer gently for 1 hour.

Put the meat and stock into a pie dish.

Roll out the pastry on a floured board and use to cover the meat — a funnel will probably be required in the centre of the dish to support the pastry.

Brush the pastry over with the beaten egg.

Make a small slit in the top of the pie for the steam to escape.

Bake in a moderately hot oven for about 35-45 minutes until golden brown.

Oven: 400°F/200°C Gas Mark 6

LOBSCOUSE OR SCOUSE

Serves 6-8

This traditional dish, usually eaten with a spoon and fork, has as many family variations as stories about its origin. Some say it was introduced to Liverpool by sailors from the many sailing ships that visited the port, and is based on a dish served aboard made from dried salt beef or pork, stewed with whatever vegetables were available, and probably thickened with dry ship's biscuits. Others claim that this economical stew was brought over by Irish immigrants. Popular in Liverpool it is believed that the nickname 'Scouse' for Liverpudlians, derives from the dish.

1½ lbs (675 g) potatoes
2 onions
1 carrot
1 swede or parsnip
1 turnip (optional)
2 lbs (900 g) shin of beef (lamb can be used instead of
   beef, or a mixture of beef and lamb)
A little seasoned flour
Salt and pepper
A pinch of mixed dried herbs
1 pint (600 ml/ 2⅔ cups) brown stock, or sufficient to
   cover
A little fat for frying
Dumplings (optional)

Peel and slice the potatoes and onions.

Peel and dice the carrots, swede or parsnip, and turnip. (The vegetables can vary according to taste and availability.)

Trim any fat off the meat and cut it into cubes.

Roll the meat in the seasoned flour.

Melt the fat in a frying pan and fry the meat and vegetables for a few minutes to seal.

Put the meat and vegetables into a saucepan.

Cover with the stock and add the herbs.

Season to taste with salt and pepper.

Bring to the boil and simmer slowly for at least 2 hours.

Dumplings can be dropped into the Lobscouse 20 minutes before the end of the cooking time (see Vegetable Broth with Dumplings).

Serve ladled into soup bowls.

BACON RIBS WITH CABBAGE

2 lbs (900 g) bacon ribs
1 medium cabbage
Vinegar for seasoning

Place the ribs in a large roasting tin.

Cover with cold water. There is no need to add salt.

Bring to the boil and simmer gently for about 2 hours on the top of the stove.

About 20 minutes before the end of the cooking time, wash the cabbage and slice it into small shreds.

Pour off sufficient water from the ribs to cover the cabbage in a saucepan.

Bring to the boil and add the shredded cabbage.

Simmer for about 15 minutes or until tender.

Strain the cabbage.

At the end of the 2 hours test the ribs with a fork. If the meat comes away from the bone it is cooked.

Remove the ribs from the tin, drain and divide into two portions.

Serve with the shredded cabbage seasoned with vinegar to taste.

POTATO ONION AND BACON BAKE   Serves 4

2 lbs (900 g) potatoes
1 lb (450 g) onions
Salt and pepper
A little milk
½ lb (225 g) bacon rashers
A little dripping

Peel and slice the potatoes.

Peel and slice the onions.

Remove the rind from the bacon.

Put alternate layers of the vegetables, starting and finishing with potato and seasoning each layer with salt and pepper to taste, into a greased baking tin or casserole dish.

Pour on a little milk.

Dot the top with small lumps of dripping.

Cook in a hot oven for about 45 minutes or until potatoes begin to brown.

Cover the top of the dish with the bacon rashers.

Continue cooking until the bacon is cooked and the potatoes are nicely brown and curling.

Oven: 375°F/190°C Gas Mark 5

BOILED LEG OF PORK

5 lb (2.25g kg) leg of pork
1 onion
1 leek
2 sage leaves
6 peppercorns
Salt and pepper

Peel the onion, and wash and prepare the leek.

Put the joint in a saucepan with enough cold water to cover it.

Add the onion, leek, sage leaves, peppercorns and seasoning to taste.

Bring slowly to the boil.

Simmer gently for about 2 hours until tender.

Serve with pease pudding, and gravy made from the stock the joint was cooked in.

LANCASTRIAN PORK LOAF

2 eggs
¼ pint (150 ml/ ⅔ cups) milk
½ lb (225 g) fresh white breadcrumbs
1 onion
½ oz (15 g) margarine
1 lb (450 g) pork sausage meat
2 cooking apples (not too sour)
½ level teaspoon of sage
Salt and pepper

Beat the eggs in a bowl, and stir in the milk and breadcrumbs.

Allow the egg mixture to stand for 30 minutes.

Peel and finely chop the onion.

Melt the margarine in a saucepan, and lightly cook the onion.

Add the pork.

Peel the apples, and grate or chop into small pieces.

Add the sage and seasoning to taste.

Stir the mixture thoroughly.

Pack into a greased loaf tin.

Bake in a moderate oven for 45 minutes until the pork loaf is firm.

Oven: 350°F/180°C Gas Mark 4

POTATO AND MEAT HASH

2 lbs (900 g) potatoes
1 lb (450 g) lean stewing beef
Salt and pepper
Stock or water to cover
½ lb (225 g) shortcrust pastry

Peel and cut the potatoes into large pieces.

Cut the meat into fairly small pieces.

Mix the meat and potato together and put into a deep pie dish — preferably a brown straight sided earthenware one as traditionally used in Lancashire.

Add enough stock or water to cover the meat and potatoes.

Season to taste with salt and pepper.

Cover the dish with a lid and cook in a slow oven for 2 hours.

Remove from the oven, and add more stock or water if required.

Roll out the pastry on a floured board to make a lid for the pie dish about ½ inch (1 cm) thick.

Put the pastry lid on the dish to cover the meat and potatoes.

Make a slit in the top for the steam to escape.

Return to the hot oven and cook for a further 25 minutes or until the pastry crust is golden brown.

Traditionally serve with pickled red cabbage.

Oven: 325°F/160°C Gas Mark 3
Increase to: 400°F/200°C Gas Mark 6

TRIPE AND ONIONS

Serves 3-4

This is a traditional Lancashire dish. It is usually served with mashed potatoes.

1 lb (450 g) dressed tripe
2 large onions
¾ pint (450 ml/ 2 cups) milk
Salt and pepper
A pinch of nutmeg (optional)
1 oz (25 g) flour or cornflour
Snippets of hot toast to garnish

Peel and slice the onions.

Wash the tripe in cold water, and then cut into pieces.

Put the tripe and onions in a saucepan and cover with the milk.

Simmer gently for 1 hour or until tender.

Drain the tripe and onions and reserve the milk.

Melt the butter in a saucepan and stir in the flour.

Cook for a few minutes to make a roux.

Gradually stir in the reserved milk and bring to the boil.

Cook gently, stirring occasionally, until the sauce thickens.

Add the tripe and onions to the sauce, and heat through before serving garnished with snippets of hot toast and mashed potatoes.

BLACK DISH

½ lb (225 g) stewing steak
1 lamb's kidney (skinned and cored)
1 black pudding
2 oz (50 g) mushrooms
1 medium onion
1 large carrot
1 level dessertspoon barley
2 level dessertspoons lentils
½ teaspoon dried sage
Salt and pepper
Water or stock to cover
1 suet dumpling per person (see Vegetable Broth with
  Suet Dumplings for method)

Cut the steak and kidney into small pieces.

Skin the black pudding and cut it up small.

Wash the mushrooms and chop.

Peel and chop the onion and carrot.

Put all the ingredients in a large ovenproof casserole dish, and add the barley, lentils, sage, and salt and pepper to taste.

Mix together.

Cover with water or stock and cook slowly for 2 hours.

Add the suet dumplings on top and cook for a further ½ hour.

Oven: 300°F/150°C Gas Mark 2

BLACK PUDDINGS

The blood and sausage skins required in this recipe can be obtained from a butcher.

8 oz (225 g) oatmeal
8 oz (225 g) suet, finely minced
A pinch of salt
2 teaspoons white pepper and 1 teaspoon black pepper
1 teaspoon powdered mint
2 pints (1.15 litres/ 4 cups) bullock's or sheep's blood
½ pint (300 ml/ 1¼ cups) skimmed milk
Sausage skins

Put the oatmeal and suet in a large bowl with the salt, pepper and mint and mix together.

Warm the milk.

Stir the blood and milk into the mixture and mix thoroughly.

Fill the sausage skins three parts full with the mixture.

Tie both ends of the skins together.

Put the puddings in a saucepan of hot water, and boil slowly for 20 minutes.

While the puddings are cooking prick each one with a pin to let the air escape.

Take out of the water and lay on a cloth to dry.

Boil the puddings again for 10 minutes when required, or cut into rounds and fry in hot fat or cook under a hot grill.

Serve with eggs and bacon for breakfast or high tea; or with a mixed grill for lunch or supper.

OATMEAL SAUSAGES

This is an old Lancashire recipe. The sausages can be made without meat.

4 oz (100 g) oatmeal
½ pint (300 ml/ 1¼ cups) water
2 oz (50 g) fat
1 oz (25 g) onion, finely grated
Salt and pepper
A pinch of nutmeg
A little cooked minced meat (optional)
Fat for frying

For the batter:
4 oz (100 g) plain flour
A pinch of salt
1 egg
¼ pint (150 ml/ ⅓ cup) milk

Melt the fat in a saucepan, and cook the onion for a few minutes.

Add the water, and bring to the boil.

Sprinkle in the oatmeal and stir until the mixture starts to boil again.

Cook slowly with the lid on the saucepan for 10 minutes.

Season to taste with the salt, pepper and nutmeg.

Stir in a little cooked minced meat if liked.

Spread the mixture on a board or plate to cool.

Roll into balls, and then make into sausage shapes.

Coat each sausage with the batter and fry in hot fat.

To make the batter:

Sieve the flour and the salt together into a bowl.

Make a well in the centre, and add the egg.

Gradually add half the milk and beat the mixture until smooth.

Add the rest of the liquid a little at a time, and continue beating until well mixed.

FRIED CHITTERLINGS WITH APPLE RINGS

Serves 4

Chitterlings are the intestines of a calf or pig. They are usually boiled before being sold. (If not prepared, they must be washed thoroughly, put in a saucepan with salted water to cover, brought to the boil, and simmered gently with the lid on for about 2 hours, or until tender).

1 lb (450 g) prepared chitterlings
Seasoned flour for coating
A pinch of powdered sage
Dripping for frying
2 cooking apples

Slice the chitterlings.

Mix the powdered sage with the seasoned flour, and use to coat the chitterlings.

Peel and core the apples with an apple corer.

Slice the apples into rings.

Melt the dripping in a frying pan, and fry the chitterlings and apple rings until golden brown.

MINT AND CURRANT PASTIES

Makes 8 pasties

The filling in these pasties is similar to Eccles Cakes, but with the unusual addition of mint.

1 lb (450 g) shortcrust pastry
2 oz (50 g) butter or margarine
4 oz (100 g) mixed peel
4 oz (100 g) currants
4 oz (100 g) brown sugar
3 oz (75 g) chopped fresh mint or to taste
A little lemon juice
A little milk
Caster sugar for sprinkling

Roll the pastry out on to a floured board, and cut out eight circles measuring about 6 inches (15 cm) in diameter.

Melt the butter or margarine in a saucepan.

Remove from the heat and stir in the mixed peel, currants, sugar and mint.

Moisten with the lemon juice.

Divide the mixture into eight equal amounts.

Put a portion on to half of each of the eight pastry circles.

Dampen the pastry edges with a little water.

Fold each circle in half over the filling to make a pasty.

Press the edges together firmly to seal.

Crimp the edges with finger and thumb or a fork.

Brush the pasties with a little milk, and sprinkle with caster sugar.

Prick each pasty with a fork.

Bake in a hot oven for 10 minutes then reduce to moderate and continue cooking for a further 15 minutes or until golden brown.

Delicious served either hot or cold.

Oven: 400°F/200°C Gas Mark 6
Reduce to: 350°F/180°C Gas Mark 4

BACON AND EGG PASTY

In the North, a pie was often called a pasty. This recipe is a forerunner of today's popular quiche. Years ago the amount of eggs used would depend upon how well the hens were laying.

8 oz (225 g) shortcrust pastry
4 oz (100 g) bacon
3 eggs
A little milk
Salt and pepper

Line an 8 inch (20 cm) pie plate with half the pastry.

Dice the bacon.

Beat the eggs well with a little milk.

Season with salt and pepper to taste.

Stir in the diced bacon.

Roll out the remainder of the pastry to make a lid.

Pour the egg mixture on to the lining.

Damp the edges with water and cover with the pastry lid.

Press the edges together to seal, and make a small hole in the centre to allow the steam to escape.

Bake in a hot oven for 10 minutes then reduce heat and continue cooking for a further 20 minutes.

Oven: 400°F/200°C Gas Mark 6
Reduce to: 350°F/180°C Gas Mark 4

POTATO AND ONION CAKES
Serves 4

1 lb (450 g) potatoes
8 oz (225 g) onions (optional)
2 oz (50 g) butter
Salt and pepper
5 oz (150 g) flour
Milk to mix
Fat for frying

Peel the potatoes.

Put in cold salted water, bring to the boil and simmer until soft.

Drain and keep hot.

Peel and grate or chop the onions finely.

Smoothly mash the potatoes, and stir in the onions.

Add the butter, seasoning to taste and 4 oz (100 g) of the flour.

Mix to a firm consistency.

Put the potato mixture on to a floured board.

Shape into small flat rounds about ¼ inch (1.5 cm) thick.

Roll the cakes in the remaining flour.

Fry in hot fat in a frying pan until brown on one side.

Turn over with a spatula and cook on the other side until golden brown.

Serve with fried bacon for breakfast; also excellent for high tea.

PEASE PUDDING

Pease pudding hot
Pease pudding cold
Pease pudding in the pot
Nine days old.

This traditional dish made from dried peas is sure to be eaten long before the nine days mentioned in the old nursery rhyme.

1 lb (450 g) green or yellow split peas
1 onion
2 sage leaves (optional)
1 oz (25 g) flour
1 oz (25 g) butter
Salt and pepper
1 egg
A pinch of nutmeg

Wash the peas and discard any black ones.

Soak them in cold water overnight.

Peel and slice the onion.

Put the drained peas in a saucepan with the onion, sage and seasoning.

Cover with warm water and bring to the boil.

Cook very slowly for about two hours, until the peas are tender, and the water absorbed.

Stir frequently during cooking taking care that they do not burn. If necessary add a little more water.

Rub the peas through a sieve or purée in a blender.

Beat the egg and use to mix the flour to a paste.

Stir into the pea purée with the butter and nutmeg.

Mix well together and check the seasoning.

Reheat gently stirring continuously, before serving.

If the pudding is being served with boiled pork or other boiled meat, it can be tied tightly in a cloth and boiled in the stock with the meat for about 30 minutes.

This will give a delicious added flavour to the pease pudding.

NODDIN' PUDDING   Serves 1

This pudding was made on Sundays for an easy tea after a huge lunch. The name comes from the fact that the family could nod off in their armchairs while waiting for their individual Puddings to cook.

4 oz (100 g) freshly cooked mashed potato
3 oz (75 g) self-raising flour
A knob of butter
A little milk to mix
Salt and pepper to taste

Add the flour to the mashed potato.

Mix thoroughly with the butter and milk.

Season with salt and pepper to taste.

Put the potato mixture into a small greased baking dish or ramekin.

Fluff the top of the potato up with a fork.

Cook in a moderate oven for 20 minutes.

Serve hot with cold roast beef and pickles.

Oven: 350°F/180°C Gas Mark 4

NETTLE PUDDING

This recipe was a particular speciality of a family who lived in the Pendle area for generations. The delicious pudding was also cooked in giant frying pans over a camp fire at the annual Nick O'Thing's charity event held in the countryside near Pendle every springtime. Today it is particularly appreciated as a tasty filler for hungry children. Like spinach, nettles 'boil down' during cooking so gather plenty.

2 onions
A large saucepanful of young nettle tops
1½ oz (40 g) butter
3 oz (75 g) porridge oats
2 eggs
Salt and pepper

Peel and slice the onions.

Wash the nettles well.

Melt 1 oz (25 g) of butter in a large saucepan and gently cook the onions for about 10 minutes, or until soft and opaque.

Add the nettles and a very little water.

Season with salt and pepper.

Cook gently for 15 minutes.

Chop the nettles in the saucepan and add ½ oz (15 g) butter.

Stir in the porridge oats.

Cook the mixture gently for about 2 minutes, stirring continuously.

Beat the eggs and stir in to the mixture.

Continue stirring over gently heat until the eggs are cooked.

Season to taste.

Serve hot with grilled bacon and tomatoes or baked beans.

APPLE SUET DUMPLINGS

For the suet pastry:
8 oz (225 g) plain flour
2 oz (50 g) shredded suet
1 oz (25 g) caster sugar
A pinch of salt
Water to mix

For the apples:
2 large baking apples (preferably Bramleys)
About 2 oz (50 g) Demerara sugar

To make the suet pastry:

Sieve the flour into a bowl and stir in the caster sugar, shredded suet and salt.

Mix with enough cold water to give a firm dough.

To make the apple dumplings:

Roll out the pastry fairly thickly on a floured board.

Cut into two circles large enough to enclose the apples.

Peel and core the apples.

Fill up each core with Demerara sugar.

Wrap the pastry around each apple.

Dampen the edges and press together firmly to seal.

Put the dumplings on a greased baking tray.

Bake in a moderately hot oven for about 45 minutes until the pastry is light and fluffy and the apples are soft when tested with a skewer.

Serve hot with custard.

Oven: 375°F/190°C Gas Mark 5

DAMSON FOOL

Fools have been popular since the Middle Ages. Gooseberries, blackberries, plums, raspberries, rhubarb or any fresh fruit can be used to make a fool in this way.

2 lbs (900 g) damsons
8 oz (225 g) caster sugar or to taste
1 pint (600 ml/ 2½ cups) milk
½ pint (300 ml/ 1¼ cups) double cream
4 egg yolks
1 tablespoon of lemon juice
A little double cream and chopped nuts for decoration

Stew the damsons with the sugar and a very little water in a saucepan over a gently heat until soft and tender.

Put the fruit through a sieve to remove the skins and stones.

Allow the fruit purée to cool.

Mix the milk and cream together and heat in a saucepan to boiling point.

Whisk the egg yolks in a separate bowl.

Pour a little of the boiling milk mixture on to the egg yolks, and continue whisking.

Pour the mixture back into the saucepan.

Stir over a low heat until the custard thickens.

Allow to cool.

Mix the damson purée with the custard and stir in the lemon juice.

Serve in one large or individual glass dishes, decorated with whipped cream and chopped nuts.

CREAMED EGG CUSTARD

Serves 8

The Broughton Park Hotel finds that guests always ask for more of this delicious speciality.

½ pint (300 ml/ 1¼ cups) milk
¼ pint (150 ml/ ⅔ cup) whipping cream
1 vanilla pod (split and with the pulp removed)
5 egg yolks
6 oz (175 g) sugar

Bring the milk, cream and vanilla pulp to boiling point in a saucepan.

Whisk the egg yolks and sugar in a separate bowl.

Add a little of the boiling milk to the sugar and yolks.

Whisk and pour all the ingredients back into the pan.

Whisk over a low heat continually until the custard thickens.

STEAMED TREACLE PUDDING

Another favourite from the Chef de Cuisine, Paul Heathcote at Broughton Park.

½ lb (225 g) butter, softened
½ lb (225 g) sugar
4 eggs
¾ lb (350 g) plain flour
1 oz (25 g) baking powder
⅛ pint (4 tablespoons/ ⅓ cup) milk
3 tablespoons golden syrup

Beat the softened butter with the sugar until white.

Add the eggs and beat in well.

Sift the flour with the baking powder and add to the mixture.

Then add the milk.

Put the golden syrup into the bottom of a greased pudding bowl, with the pudding mixture on top.

Cover with foil and steam for one hour.

FIG PUDDING

Figs were frequently used in old Lancashire recipes, and fig pudding was especially popular. Most of the fruit was imported from Spain through the busy port of Liverpool.

½ lb (225 g) figs
4 oz (100 g) shredded suet
4 oz (100 g) plain flour
6 oz (175 g) granulated sugar
4 oz (100 g) breadcrumbs
½ teaspoon bicarbonate of soda
½ teaspoon cream of tartar
A pinch of salt
2 eggs
About 2 fl oz (3 tablespoons/ ¼ cup) buttermilk or milk

Chop the figs into small pieces.

Mix the suet, flour, sugar, breadcrumbs, bicarbonate of soda, cream of tartar and salt together well.

Beat the eggs, and add the buttermilk or milk.

Use the liquid to mix the dry ingredients to a soft consistency.

Put the mixture into a greased pudding basin. Use a sufficiently large basin to only fill three-quarters with the mixture, as the pudding will swell during cooking. Tie down with a pudding cloth or make a foil lid.

Steam for at least 2 hours.

Turn out on to a serving dish.

Excellent accompanied by either white sauce or custard.

LANCASHIRE CHRISTMAS PUDDING PIES

Left-over Christmas pudding was often used up as a rich mincemeat, and cooked in pies. These were traditionally eaten hot for high tea. If preferred the pie may be made in one baking tin, and served cut into fingers.

Left-over Christmas pudding
Butter
A little brandy or rum
Short or puff pastry
White of egg or milk
Caster sugar

Mash the cold left-over pudding with enough butter to make a smooth consistency.

Flavour with a little brandy or rum to taste.

Line greased patty tins with the pastry.

Put a spoonful of pudding mixture on to each pastry round.

Dampen the edges with cold water.

Cut sufficient pastry rounds for lids.

Put the lids on the pies, pressing the edges together firmly.

Make a small hole in the top of each pie, and brush with white of egg or milk.

Dredge generously with caster sugar.

Bake in a hot oven for 20 minutes, or until golden brown.

Serve hot.

STICKY TOFFEE PUDDING

Serves 8

6 oz (175 g) butter
6 oz (175 g) golden syrup
6 oz (175 g) soft brown sugar
Thick slices of one-day-old white bread — probably
   about 3 will be required although the quantity does
   depend on the size of the loaf
A little milk

Cut the bread into slices about 1 inch (2.5 cm) thick.

Take off the crust and cut each slice into fingers about 3-4 inches (7.5cm - 10 cm) long and 1-1½ inches (2.5cm - 3.5 cm) wide. Eight fingers will be required in all.

Melt the butter, sugar and syrup in a frying pan, and continue cooking until thick, brown and toffee-like.

Dip the bread fingers into the milk.

Fry the bread in the butter, sugar and syrup mixture for several minutes basting occasionally.

Arrange the slices on a serving dish and pour on the toffee sauce.

Serve with whipped cream.

51

JACK TART

6 oz (175 g) shortcrust pastry
Raspberry jam
2 oz (50 g) margarine
2 oz (50 g) sugar
4 oz (100 g) rolled oats

Roll out the pastry on a floured board.

Use to line a greased ovenproof tart plate.

Spread the pastry with a layer of raspberry jam, leaving ½ inch (1 cm) or so free round the each.

Melt the margarine and sugar in a saucepan, and stir in the oats. Mix well.

Spread the mixture evenly on top of the jam.

Decorate the edge of the tart with a fork, or crimp with finger and thumb.

Bake in a moderate oven for 30 minutes or until golden brown.

Oven: 375°F/190°C Gas Mark 5

MANCHESTER TART

8 oz (225 g) shortcrust pastry
About 2 oz (50 g) jam
1 egg
½ pint (300 ml/ 1¼ cups) milk
A little caster sugar
A pinch of salt
A little powdered cinnamon or nutmeg (optional)

Roll out the pastry on a floured board, and use to line a greased shallow pie dish.

Cover the pastry with a layer of jam.

Mix the egg with the milk.

Add sugar and salt to taste.

Beat together until well mixed.

Pour the milk mixture into the pastry case.

Sprinkle a little cinnamon or nutmeg on the top, if liked.

Bake in a hot oven for 30 minutes until golden brown and set.

Serve hot or cold.

Oven: 425°F/220°C Gas Mark 7

TREACLE TART

For centuries sugar and molasses were imported from the West Indies and other places, through the busy port of Liverpool, and the use of treacle has been popular in Lancashire cooking. It was also used to sweeten breakfast porridge.

6 oz (175 g) plain flour
A pinch of salt
3 oz (75 g) butter or margarine
About 3 tablespoonsful of cold water
6 oz (175 g) golden syrup
1 tablespoonful black treacle
The juice and finely grated rind of 1 lemon
8 oz (225 g) white breadcrumbs
2 tablespoonsful sour cream
A pinch of nutmeg

Sieve the flour and salt into a bowl.

Rub in the butter or margarine until the mixture resembles fine breadcrumbs.

Mix with sufficient cold water to make a firm dough.

Wrap the pastry in greaseproof paper and leave to cool and rest for 30 minutes.

Heat the syrup, treacle, lemon juice and rind in a saucepan until melted.

Stir in the nutmeg.

Remove from the heat, and allow to cool a little.

Stir the breadcrumbs and soured cream into the mixture.

Pour the filling into the pastry case.

Bake in a moderate oven for about 20 minutes until firm.

Serve hot or cold with whipped cream.

Oven: 375°F/190°C Gas Mark 5

TREACLE TOFFEE

Everton is famous for a type of toffee. Everton toffee was first made by Molly Bushell (1736-1813) in what was then a small town, and is now part of the city of Liverpool. Everton is so well known for toffee that formerly the townspeople and now the members of Everton Football Club are known as Everton Toffeemen. Molly Bushell has become the mascot of the Everton Supporters Club, depicted in their badge.

1 lb (450 g) Demerara sugar
8 oz (225 g) black treacle
4 oz (100 g) butter
1 tablespoon of vinegar
1 tablespoon of water

Put the sugar, black treacle, butter, vinegar and water into a thick saucepan.

Dissolve the sugar over a low heat stirring with a wooden spoon.

Bring to the boil, and boil rapidly without stirring for 10-15 minutes. The temperature should reach 280°F/140°C, but to test without a sugar thermometer drop a little toffee into a saucer of cold water. If it hardens, the toffee is ready.

Remove from the heat.

Pour the toffee into a greased tin and leave to set.

Mark into squares just before setting point is reached.

NUTMEG SPONGE

8 oz (225 g) margarine
8 oz (225 g) Demerara sugar
8 oz (225 g) flour
2 teaspoons baking powder
2 teaspoons nutmeg
4 eggs

For the vanilla butter cream icing:
3 oz (75 g) butter or margarine
6 oz (175 g) icing sugar
Vanilla essence

Sieve the flour, baking powder and nutmeg into a bowl.

In another bowl cream the margarine and sugar together until light and fluffy.

Beat in the eggs one at a time.

Gradually fold in the flour mixture.

Mix to a soft dropping consistency.

Divide the mixture evenly between two greased sandwich tins.

Bake in a moderate oven for 25 minutes until firm and golden brown.

When the cakes are cool, sandwich together with vanilla butter cream icing.

To make the vanilla cream icing:

Sieve the icing sugar into a bowl.

In another bowl cream the butter or margarine until very pale in colour.

Gradually add the icing sugar a little at a time.

Add the vanilla essence to taste.

Beat until the icing is smooth and creamy.

Oven: 350°F/180°C   Gas Mark 4

DIET BREAD CAKE

Sponge cakes were always made in this manner before chemical raising agents became available.

4 eggs
8 oz (225 g) caster sugar
A pinch of caraway seeds
1 teaspoonful ground ginger (optional)
1 lemon (optional)
1 orange (optional)
6 oz (175 g) plain flour
Caster sugar for dusting or glacé icing if preferred

Whisk the eggs and sugar in an electric mixer or a bowl standing in hot water until thick and creamy.

Fold in the caraway seeds.

Mix in the ginger, or if preferred, the finely grated rind of a lemon and orange.

Sieve the flour and gently fold it into the mixture a little at a time using a metal spoon.

Put the mixture into a greased cake tin.

Bake in a moderate oven for 40 minutes.

Either dust with caster sugar before baking or leave to cool after removing from the oven and then decorate the cake with glacé icing.

Oven: 375°F/190°C   Gas Mark 5

GOOSNARGH CAKES

Makes about 16

These delicious sweet shortbread cakes come from a village near Preston.

8 oz (225 g) plain flour
6 oz (175 g) butter
About 2½ oz (65 g) caster sugar
1 teaspoonful caraway seeds

Sieve the flour into a bowl.

Rub in the fat until the mixture resembles fine breadcrumbs.

Stir in about 1½ oz (40 g) of sugar and the caraway seeds.

Knead the mixture into a soft dough.

Roll out on a floured board to about ½ inch (1 cm) thick.

Cut into rounds with a medium cutter.

Sprinkle each cake with caster sugar pressing it in a little.

Put the cakes on a greased baking sheet and leave to rest for a few hours or overnight.

Bake in a slow oven for about 25 minutes until pale cream in colour.

Oven: 300°F/150°C Gas Mark 2

ECCLES CAKES

Eccles was very famous for its Wakes Celebrations. The fun started on the Sunday after the 25th August and lasted for four days. Entertainments, races and competitions included bull baiting, apple dumpling eating (with a 5s. prize for the first to finish), catching a pig and a fiddling competition.

Traditional Lancashire Eccles cakes are made from shortcrust, not flaky pastry.

½ lb (225 g) shortcrust pastry
3 oz (75 g) sugar
½ teaspoon ground mixed spice
1 oz (25 g) finely chopped mixed peel
½ lb (225 g) currants
A knob of margarine or butter
1 tablespoon of water

Roll out the pastry on a floured board.

Cut into rounds using a saucer as a template.

Damp all round the edges of the pastry.

Put the currants, sugar, spice, peel and margarine in a bowl and mix well.

Put a tablespoon of the mixture on to each round and gather the edges together over the top.

Press the edges together to seal.

Turn the cakes over and roll or press down slightly, so that the filling begins to show through.

Make two small slits in the top of each cake.

Put the cakes on a greased baking sheet.

Bake in a hot oven for 20 minutes.

Oven: 425°F/220°C Gas Mark 7

BURY SIMNEL CAKE

This rich fruit cake, a speciality of the Bury region, dates back to the Middle Ages, and has a religious significance. It was baked on Simnel Sunday — the 4th Sunday in Lent — now known as Mothering Sunday, as a welcome indulgence in the middle of the season of fasting and abstinence. The day became one on which many servants in grand houses were allowed to visit home, and were permitted to bake a cake for the occasion.

The cake is traditionally decorated with eleven balls of almond paste to represent the Disciples, omitting Judas, with a ring of icing in the centre filled with marzipan spring flowers, like violets and primroses. If the cake is intended for Easter time, chickens and coloured eggs are often placed in the centre.

8 oz (225 g) butter or margarine
8 oz (225 g) brown sugar
4 eggs
8 oz (225 g) currants
8 oz (225 g) sultanas
3 oz (75 g) mixed candied peel, chopped
8 oz (225 g) plain flour
1 teaspoonful of mixed spice, ground cinnamon and
  ground nutmeg
2 teaspoonsful baking powder
2 oz (50 g) black treacle
2 oz (50 g) ground almonds
1 tablespoonful of rum or brandy (optional)
A little milk to mix if required

For the almond paste: makes 1½ lbs (675 g)
8 oz (225 g) caster sugar
8 oz (225 g) icing sugar
12 oz (350 g) ground almonds
1 teaspoon vanilla essence
2 small eggs

Cream the butter and sugar until pale and fluffy.

Whisk the eggs together and gradually beat them into the creamed mixture a little at a time.

In a separate bowl sieve together the plain flour, baking powder, spices and ground almonds.

In another bowl mix the currants, sultanas and candied peel.

Fold in half of the flour mixture to the creamed butter.

Add the dried fruit and stir in the treacle.

Fold in the rest of the flour mixture, and add the rum or brandy, if liked.

Mix to a soft dropping consistency adding a little milk if required.

Pour half the mixture in a greased and lined 8 inch (20 cm) round cake tin, and level the top.

To make the almond paste:

Sieve the icing sugar into a bowl and add the caster sugar and the ground almonds.

Stir in the vanilla essence.

Beat the eggs and use sufficient to mix to a stiff paste.

Roll into a ball and knead lightly.

Divide the almond paste into three.

Roll out one third of the paste into a circle to fit the cake tin about ½ inch (1 cm) thick.

Lay the almond paste circle on top of the cake mixture in the tin.

Put the remaining cake mixture in the tin and level the top.

Bake in a moderate oven for 1 hour, lower the heat to cool and cook for a further 2 hours or until golden brown and firm to the touch.

Allow to cool before removing from the tin.

Roll out the second third of the almond paste to fit the top of the cake.

Brush the top of the cake with a little melted apricot jam.

Gently press on the almond paste circle.

Make eleven small balls from the remaining paste, and press them gently into position round the edge of the cake.

Beat the egg yolk and use it to brush the top of the cake, including the almond paste balls.

Put the cake back into a very hot oven for about 5 minutes to lightly brown the egg.

When the cake is cold decorate the centre as desired.

Oven: 325°F/160°C Gas Mark 3
Reduce to: 300°F/150°C Gas Mark 2
Increase to: 450°F/230°C Gas Mark 8

CHORLEY CAKES

1 lb (450 g) shortcrust pastry
12 oz (350 g) currants
4 oz (100 g) caster sugar (or more if liked)
4 oz (100 g) butter or margarine
A little milk to glaze.

Roll out the pastry on a floured board.

Cut out four rounds the size of a tea plate.

Put 2 oz (50 g) of currants in the centre of each pastry circle. Spread out evenly.

Sprinkle with 1 oz (25 g) of sugar and dot with 1 oz (25 g) of fat cut into small pieces.

Damp the edge of each circle with a little water.

Draw the dampened edges together and press to seal.

Turn the cakes over and roll out again to about ¾ inch (1.5 cm) thick, keeping the same round shape, until the currants begin to show through the pastry.

Score each cake three times with a knife.

Brush over the tops with the milk.

Put on to a greased baking sheet and cook in a hot oven for about 25 minutes until golden brown.

Spread each cake with butter before serving.

THURSDAY CAKE

Although this cake was traditionally eaten on Thursdays, it is just as good on any day of the week.

12 oz (350 g) plain flour
A pinch of salt
1 level teaspoonful of mixed spice
6 oz (175 g) lard
6 oz (175 g) sugar
12 oz (350 g) mixed dried fruit
2 level teaspoonsful of bicarbonate of soda
1 pint (600 ml/ 2½ cups) milk
½ pint (300 ml/ 1¼ cups) water
2 tablespoonsful of vinegar

Sift together the flour, salt and mixed spice into a bowl.

Rub in the lard until the mixture resembles fine breadcrumbs.

Mix the milk and water together.

Dissolve the bicarbonate of soda in a little of the milk and water mixture.

Make a well in the flour mixture and stir in the milk and water, and the vinegar.

Mix well to a dropping consistency.

Put the mixture into a greased cake tin.

Bake in the oven for 1¾-2 hours until well risen and golden brown.

Oven: 325°F/160°C Gas Mark 3

SALLY CAKE

This is a very old Lancashire recipe, possibly a favourite of the 'Sally from our Alley', made famous by singer Gracie Fields, the well-loved 'Lassie from Lancashire' who was born in Rochdale in 1898.

4 oz (100 g) brown sugar
4 oz (100 g) raisins
2 oz (50 g) butter
8 oz (225 g) plain flour
8 fl oz (250 ml/ 1 cup) water
1 teaspoon ground nutmeg
1 teaspoon cinnamon
½ teaspoon salt
5 level teaspoons baking powder

Put the butter, raisins, spices and water in a saucepan.

Bring to the boil and continue boiling for 2 minutes.

Allow to cool.

Sieve the flour and baking powder together and fold into the mixture to give a soft dropping consistency.

Put into a lined greased cake tin.

Bake in a moderate oven for 1 hour until well risen and golden brown.

Oven: 325°F/160°C Gas Mark 3

TOSSET CAKES

It used to be the custom in Lancashire for Tosset cakes to be eaten between slices of buttered bread at funerals, accompanied by homemade blackberry wine.

8 oz (225 g) plain flour
4 oz (100 g) butter
1 oz (25 g) caster sugar
¼ teaspoon of cinnamon

Cream the butter and sugar until light and fluffy.

Sieve the flour and cinnamon together, and fold into the mixture.

Mix to a soft dough.

Roll out thinly on a floured board.

Cut out with a cutter and put on a greased baking sheet.

Bake in a hot oven for 20 minutes or until golden brown.

Oven: 400°F/200°C Gas Mark 6

OATCAKES

Oatcakes have been sold in Blackburn market for over fifty years. The popularity of these delicious biscuits dates back over centuries. Traditionally they were made in an oblong shape about 6 inch (15 cm) long and 3 inches (7.5 cm) wide, achieved by throwing the oat dough from a cup on to a hot greased tray before baking.

8 oz (225 g) fine oatmeal
4 oz (100 g) self raising flour
A pinch of salt
½ teaspoon of bicarbonate of soda
2 oz (50 g) margarine
1 egg
Milk to mix

Sieve the flour, salt and bicarbonate of soda in a bowl.

Rub in the fat until the mixture resembles fine breadcrumbs.

Add the oatmeal and rub altogether.

Mix in the beaten egg and sufficient milk to give a stiff dough.

Put on a board sprinkled with oatmeal.

Roll out with a rolling pin or flatten with a hand to about ¼ inch (5 mm) thick.

Rub the dough over with more oatmeal.

Cut into rounds with a pastry cutter.

Put the oatcakes on a greased baking sheet.

Bake in a moderate oven for 10 minutes.

Spread with butter and serve with cheese or preserve; or plain with bacon and egg.

Oven: 350°F/180°C Gas Mark 4

SAD CAKE

This pastry 'cake' was particularly popular in the villages of Rossendale and was also made in Blackburn fifty years ago.

8 oz (225 g) plain flour
A pinch of salt
4 oz (100 g) lard
Cold water to mix

Sieve the flour into a bowl with the salt.

Rub the lard into the flour until the mixture resembles fine breadcrumbs.

Mix to a soft dough with cold water.

Roll out the pastry on a floured board about ¼ inch (5 mm) thick.

Shape into a flat round, and put on a greased baking sheet.

Cook in a hot oven for about 10-15 minutes. Do not overcook, Sad Cake should be soft and doughy.

Eat while still warm, spread with butter alone or butter and jam.

Oven: 375°F/190°C Gas Mark 5

Cup and Saucer.

FARMHOUSE CAKE

1 lb (450 g) plain flour
6 oz (175 g) sugar
8 oz (225 g) sultanas
8 oz (225 g) lard
**1 teaspoonful of bicarbonate of soda, dissolved in
 a little water**
½ pint (300 ml/ 1¼ cups) hot milk
2 teaspoonsful of vinegar

Sieve the flour into a bowl.

Rub in the lard until the mixture resembles fine breadcrumbs.

Stir in the sugar and sultanas.

Add the milk, vinegar and bicarbonate of soda.

Mix to a dropping consistency.

Put the mixture into a greased cake tin.

Bake for 1½-2 hours until well risen and golden brown.

Oven: 375°F/190°C Gas Mark 5

Tea Pot

OLD FASHIONED HERMITS

Makes 24

From a handwritten recipe book dated about 1870 belonging to a lady who lived in Oldham. She worked in a cotton mill at one time and was taught to read and write by her husband — a teacher at the Ragged School, Preston.

12 oz (350 g) flour
6 oz (175 g) brown sugar
4 oz (100 g) butter or dripping
2 eggs
2 fl oz (3 tablespoons/ ¼ cup) milk
1 level teaspoon of bicarbonate of soda
2 tablespoonfuls of treacle
2 teaspoonsful of powdered cinnamon
1 teaspoonful of cloves
A pinch of grated nutmeg
A little flour
4 oz (100 g) chopped raisins

Sieve the flour into a large mixing bowl.

Stir the brown sugar, and the softened fat.

Beat the eggs, and add to the mixture.

Stir the bicarbonate of soda into the milk, and add the treacle, cinnamon, cloves and nutmeg.

Roll the raisins in the extra flour and stir them into the mixture.

Mix well together to a firm dropping consistency.

Put the mixture in small spoonfuls on greased baking sheets allowing room for spreading during cooking.

Bake in a moderate oven for 20 minutes.

Oven: 350°F/180°C Gas Mark 4

OLD TIME GINGERBREAD

Gingerbread, biscuits and parkins are popular throughout Lancashire. In a 19th century song about Ormskirk one verse states:

> 'Ormskirk is a funny little town
> And long ago was said
> To be celebrated for old maids
> As well as gingerbread.'

6 oz (175 g) self-raising or plain flour
2 oz (50 g) margarine
1 oz (25 g) caster sugar
2 tablespoons golden syrup
½ teaspoon ground ginger
A pinch of salt
Milk to mix

Sieve the flour into a bowl.

Rub the margarine into the flour until the mixture resembles fine breadcrumbs.

Add the sugar, syrup, bicarbonate of soda, ginger, and salt.

Mix with the milk to a smooth consistency.

Put the mixture into a well greased tin.

Bake in a slow oven for 30 minutes or until firm to the touch.

Oven: 350°F/180°C Gas Mark 4

MIDDLEFORTH AND PENWORTHAM BUNNOCK OR PARKIN

Middleforth, near Preston, has its own parkin recipe. Parkin is similar to gingerbread but has the addition of oatmeal. It is believed that this recipe dates from the turn of the century when barrels of treacle were delivered to shops by horse and cart, and housewives used to send their children with a jam-jar to fill up.

Local legend recounts that on one day the horse and cart had reached the top of Pear Tree Brow when the treacle barrels fell off and rolled down the hill, where they split open. The villagers helped themselves to jar after jar of treacle and made great quantities of Bunnock and toffee, as well as enjoying it on their breakfast porridge.

When the Bunnock was sold in the village shops it was baked in huge slabs. Villagers bought it by the pound, and the required amount was cut from the slab by two forks.

½ lb (225 g) medium oatmeal
4 oz (100 g) plain flour
2 teaspoons ground ginger
4 oz (100 g) margarine
6 oz (175 g) sugar
½ lb (225 g) treacle
½ teaspoon bicarbonate of soda
A little milk
1 egg

Mix the oatmeal, flour and ground ginger together in a bowl.

Melt the margarine, sugar and treacle in a saucepan, and add to the dry ingredients.

Mix the bicarbonate of soda with a little milk.

Add with the egg to the mixture.

Beat well together.

Spoon the mixture into a well greased shallow baking tin about 8 inches (20 cm) square.

Bake in a slow oven for 1½ hours.

Remove from the oven and allow to cool in the tin.

When cold, cut the Bunnock into squares.

Oven: 300°F/150°C Gas Mark 2

RAISIN TEA BREAD

Another recipe of the Preston Schoolmaster's wife dating from 1870.

10 oz (275 g) flour
¼ oz (20 g) baking powder
¼ oz (20 g) bicarbonate of soda
3 oz (75 g) butter
6 oz (175 g) sugar
1 egg
4 oz (100 g) raisins
A pinch of nutmeg
A little milk to mix

Sieve the flour, baking powder and bicarbonate of soda into a bowl.

In a separate bowl, cream the butter and sugar, and beat in the egg.

Fold the flour into the butter mixture.

Stir in the raisins and the nutmeg.

Mix to a dropping consistency with a little milk.

Spoon the mixture into a greased 1 lb (450 g) loaf tin.

Bake in a moderate oven for 1 hour or until golden brown.

Serve sliced, plain or buttered.

Oven: 350°F/180°C Gas Mark 4

LANCASHIRE CHEESE SCONES Makes 10-12

½ lb (225 g) self-raising flour
3 oz (75 g) margarine
3 oz (75 g) Lancashire cheese, crumbled
¼ pint (150 ml/ ⅔ cup) milk
Salt to taste

Sieve the flour and salt into a bowl.

Rub in the margarine until the mixture resembles fine breadcrumbs.

Add the cheese.

Mix into a soft dough with the milk.

Roll out the pastry on a floured board to about 2 inch (5 cm) thick.

Stamp into rounds with a cutter.

Bake in a hot oven for 10-15 minutes, until well risen and golden brown.

Serve either hot or cold, split and spread with butter.

Oven: 425°F/220°C Gas Mark 7

MUFFINS

1 lb (450 g) plain flour
½ teaspoon salt
½ oz (15 g) fresh yeast
1 oz (25 g) caster sugar
1 egg, beaten
7 fl oz (200 ml/ 3 cups) tepid water

Sieve the flour and the salt together.

Cream the yeast with the sugar.

Stir the yeast mixture into a little of the warmed water.

Add the beaten egg and pour on to the flour.

Mix in sufficient of the remaining water to form a soft dough.

Knead well.

Cover the top of the bowl and leave in a warm place for 1½ hours or until risen to double in size.

Roll the dough out on a floured board to a thickness of about ¾ inch (1.5 cm).

Cut into rounds about 3 inches (7.5 cm) in diameter.

Put on a greased baking tray, and bake in a hot oven for about 15 minutes.

After about 7 minutes of the cooking time, turn the muffins over with a slice, and then continue cooking on the other side.

Allow the muffins to cool.

Toast under a grill before serving hot, spread with butter.

Oven: 425°F/220°C Gas Mark 7

PICKLED RED CABBAGE

Pickled red cabbage is traditionally served with Lancashire Hotpot.

A few drops of cochineal can be added to the vinegar prior to boiling for a pretty appearance. Because of the vinegar, use an aluminium, stainless steel or enamelled saucepan and not a brass, copper or iron one when making pickles or chutneys. Also use a wooden spoon for mixing.

For the pickled red cabbage:
3 lbs (1.5 kg) red cabbage
1 lb (450 g) onions
3 oz (75 g) cooking salt
Approximately 2 pints (1.15 litres/ 4 cups) spiced vinegar

For the spiced* vinegar:
2 pints (1.15 litres/ 4 cups) white wine vinegar
1 oz (25 g) blade mace
½ oz (15 g) ground ginger
½ oz (15 g) whole allspice
½ oz (15 g) cloves
6 peppercorns
1 cinnamon stick

* If preferred 2 oz (50 g) of pickling spice can be used instead of the individual spices.

To make the spiced vinegar:

Put the vinegar and spices into a saucepan.

Bring to the boil and pour into a bowl.

Allow to cool, cover the bowl and leave for at least 2 hours or longer if a stronger flavour is liked.

Strain the vinegar, and use as required.

To make the pickled red cabbage:

Remove the tough outside leaves from the cabbage.

Shred the rest of the cabbage finely.

Peel and slice the onions.

Put the cabbage and onions in layers in a bowl, sprinkling each layer with the salt.

Cover and leave for 24 hours.

Drain.

Pack the vegetables loosely into jars, to come to one inch from the top, and cover with cold spiced vinegar, leaving ½ inch space at the top.

Cover with a metal lid with a vinegar proof lining, greaseproof paper or calico dipped in melted paraffin wax or candle grease. Secure tightly to prevent the vinegar evaporating.

Store in a cool, dry, dark place.

Keep for 2 or 3 weeks before using for the flavour to develop.

Unlike other pickles, cabbage is best not stored for too long, otherwise it loses its delicious crispness.

SHEEP'S BRAIN SANDWICH SPREAD

1 sheep's brain
1 tablespoonful of vinegar
A knob of butter
Salt and pepper
1 hard-boiled egg

Soak the brain in cold salted water, then wash thoroughly and remove any bone and blood.

Put in a saucepan of fresh salted water to which the vinegar has been added, and boil for 20 minutes.

Strain.

Mash the brain with a fork, pass through a sieve, or blend in an electric mixer.

Add salt and pepper to taste, the knob of butter and the mashed hard-boiled egg.

Allow to cool.

Put the spread into small pots and cover.

Delicious as a sandwich spread, or serve on toast.

How to Pickle Cockles

Hang them in Pan over the fire till they open, when they are opened Pick them out of the shells then wash them very well in salt & Water then put them in a sive to dry, then take some good Elleker boyl it with a Handfull of Salt and a little of the Pickle that came from them in the Pan when it is cleared with a few Cloves Pepper Corns Race Ginger & 2 or 3 Cloves when your Pickle is cold put your Cockles into it & cover them very close up in Earthen Potts.

SHRIMP SAUCE

1 pint (600 ml/ 2½ cups) cooked shrimps weighed in
 their shells
1 oz (25 g) margarine or butter
1 oz (25 g) plain flour
½ pint (300 ml/ 1¼ cups) milk
Salt and pepper
1 teaspoon anchovy essence (or the juice of ½ a lemon,
 if preferred)

Shell the shrimps.

Melt the fat in a saucepan.

Stir in the flour to make a roux.

Cook for a minute still stirring.

Gradually stir in the milk.

Bring to the boil, and simmer for a few minutes until the
sauce thickens, still stirring.

Season with salt and pepper.

Add the shrimps.

Stir in the anchovy essence or lemon juice.

Cook gently for a few minutes to allow the shrimps to heat
through before serving.

RHUBARB CHUTNEY

2 lbs (900 g) rhubarb
2 lemons
1 oz (25 g) root ginger
1 oz (25 g) garlic
2 lbs (900 g) Demerara sugar
A good pinch of cayenne pepper
1 oz (25 g) salt
1 lb (450 g) sultanas
1 pint (600 ml/ 2½ cups) malt vinegar

Wash the rhubarb and cut each stalk into small pieces.

Put it into a bowl.

Squeeze the lemons and pour the juice over the rhubarb.

Bruise the ginger and tie it in a muslin bag.

Chop the garlic into small pieces.

Put the rhubarb and lemon, sugar, pepper, salt, sultanas, garlic and vinegar into a preserving pan.

Add the bag of ginger.

Bring to the boil, and simmer, stirring frequently until the mixture is tender and becomes thick. This may take 1-1½ hours.

Remove the bag of ginger.

Pour into dry, clean jars and cover with purchased jam covers, then with a round cloth, brushed with melted candle grease to make an air-tight seal.

Store for a month before using.

LEMON CHEESE

4 oz (100 g) butter
2 eggs
8 oz (225 g) lump or granulated sugar
Grated zest and juice of 2 lemons

Put all the ingredients into a fireproof jug or basin.

Stand in a pan of constantly simmering hot water.

Stir in the mixture continuously for about 20 minutes until it sets into lemon cheese.

Put into a warmed dry jar and cover tightly.

Lemon cheese can be kept in a refrigerator for up to two weeks.

Champaign Ice

Mix a bottle of champaign with a pint of rich lemon ice, sweeten it to your taste put it in the freezer, and work it well. Any kind of wine may be used in the same manner.

Mrs. Owen 1854.

NETTLE BEER

This recipe has been handed down through the generations. When a lad in the second half of the 19th century, May Aunger's grandfather used to set off on adventures during the school holidays carrying a quart bottle of his grandmother's homemade nettle beer under his arm. 'Marvalous stuff', he called it.

2 lbs (900 g) of nettle tops, gathered while wearing gloves
2 lemons
8 oz (225 g) brown sugar
8 pints (4.5 litres) water
1 oz (25 g) cream of tartar
½ oz (15 g) yeast

Wash the nettle leaves well, while wearing gloves.

Put into a saucepan of boiling water, and simmer for 30 minutes.

Grate the rind and squeeze the juice from the lemons.

Strain the nettle liquid into a large bowl.

Add the lemon rind and juice, sugar and cream of tartar, while stirring.

Allow to cool.

Add the yeast.

Cover the bowl and leave in a warm place for three days.

Strain the nettle beer and pour it into strong clean screw top beer bottles.

Keep for one week before drinking.

BLACKBERRY WINE

Makes 4 pints

3 lbs (1.5 kg) blackberries
1 lb (450 g) granulated sugar
4 pints (2.25 litres/ 8 cups) cold water

Choose large ripe blackberries to make the wine.

Wash and prepare the fruit.

Put the water in a saucepan, and bring it to the boil.

Add the fruit, and boil for 10 minutes.

Strain.

Put the blackberry juice and the sugar in a bowl.

Leave to ferment for 10 days.

Take off any scum that has formed.

Strain.

Bottle the wine, and leave for 6 months before drinking.

To Give Shirts Fronts a Gloss and Look of Newness

In the Lancashire Record Office among unpublished handwritten recipes and remedies of 17th century origin, there are also methods for making tooth powder and furniture varnish, and this one . . .

Take 2 oz of fine white gum arabac powder, put it into a pitcher & pour on a pint or More of boiling water, according to degree of strength you desire, then having covered it, let it stand all night, in the Morning pour carefully the clear liquid from the dregs, into a clean bottle, cork it, and keep it for use, a tablespoonful of gum water, stirred into a pint of starch Made in the usual Manner, this will produce a gloss which nothing can surpass.

Grateful thanks are extended to the many people of Lancashire who have contributed towards the collection of recipes, in particular:

The Lancashire Record Office, Preston, for To give Shirt Fronts a Gloss and Look of Newness, Champaign Ice, and How to Pickle Cockles.

Paul Heathcote, Chef de Cuisine, Broughton Park Hotel, Preston, for Goosnargh Chicken with Wild Mushroom Sauce, Treacle Pudding and Creamed Egg Custard.

Geoffrey Beetlestone, Head Chef of the Inn at Whitewell, Forest of Bowland, near Clitheroe, for Pheasant in Puff Pastry with Wild Mushrooms.

Molly Ingham of Silverdale for Nettle Pudding.

Hilda Scattergood of Rochdale for Potato, Onion and Bacon Bake and Bacon and Egg Pasty.

Joan Holden of Preston for Lemon Cheese.

Phyllis Jorden of Birkby, Huddersfield, Yorkshire, for Rhubarb Chutney, Thursday Cake and Farmhouse Cake.

Ida Wilkinson of Warrington for Bacon Ribs and Cabbage, Vegetable Broth and Dumplings, Lancashire Hot Pot, Manchester Tart and Apple Dumplings.

Elsie Spencer of Southport for Noddin Pudding.

Kathleen Anderson of Southport for Oatcakes, Lobscouse and Sad Cake.

May Aunger of Colne for Black Puddings, Nettle Beer, Old time Gingerbread, Jack Tart, Oatmeal Sausages, Nutmeg Sponge, Sally Cake, Treacle Tart, and Fig Pudding.

Edna Cattermole of Preston for Bury Simnel Cake, Chorley Cakes and Middleforth and Penwortham Bunnock or Parkin.

Hessie Holden of Stockport for Raisin Tea Bread and Old Fashioned Hermits.

Joy Caunce of Milnthorpe for Stewed Steak and Cow-heel.

Barbara Corless of Liverpool for Pea and Lentil Soup and Barley Soup.

Geoffrey Akroyd of Ashton under Lyme for Mint and Currant Pasties, Ginger Wine, and information.

Joan and Carol Mulvaney for help and information.

THE COUNTRY RECIPE SERIES

Available now @ £1.95 each

Cambridgeshire
Cornwall
Cumberland & Westmorland
Devon
Dorset
Hampshire
Kent
Lancashire
Norfolk
Somerset
Sussex
Yorkshire

Coming September 1988

Leicestershire
Oxfordshire
Suffolk
Warwickshire

All these books are available at your local bookshop or newsagent, or can be ordered direct from the publisher. Just tick the titles you require and fill in the form below. Prices and availability subject to change without notice.

Ravette Books Limited, 3 Glenside Estate, Star Road, Partridge Green, Horsham, West Sussex RH13 8RA.

Please send a cheque or postal order, and allow the following for postage and packing. UK 25p for one book and 10p for each additional book ordered.

Name ....

Address ....

....

....